YOLANDA SCOTT

CHOSEN

How to answer the call of greatness that is upon your life

YOLANDA SCOTT

CHOSEN

How to answer the call of greatness that is upon your life

T&J PUBLISHERS

A SMALL INDEPENDENT PUBLISHER WITH A BIG VOICE

Printed in the United States of America by
T&J Publishers (Atlanta, GA.)
www.TandJPublishers.com

All Scriptures are from the King James Version (KJV) and the New English Translation (NET).

Cover design by Jazmine Rochelle (JRE Creative)
Book format and layout by Timothy Flemming, Jr. (T&J Publishers)

ISBN: 978-0-9981621-6-4

To contact author, go to:
www.YolandaCScott.com
PastorYCScott@gmail.com
Facebook: Yolanda C. Scott
Facebook: Yolanda C. Scott Ministry
Instagram: YolondaCScottMinistry

ACKNOWLEDGMENTS

First, I would like to thank the Lord Jesus Christ for entrusting me with such a powerful message for His people.

To my wonderful husband, my pastor, and my friend, Edward Demetrics Scott, thank you for all that you have pushed and encouraged me to become and accomplish. There is absolutely no way I could have accomplished any of my endowments without you.

To my wonderful children, Tremonte, Vernisha, Robert, Isaiah, and my son-in-law Jeremiah, I truly thank each of you for all of your love and continual encouragement toward me! I love each of you. Now go and follow the path that has been given to you.

To my granddaughter, little Zayniah Joy, granny loves you and appreciate you!! I thank God everyday for giving you to me, little sunshine. Your presence brings me much JOY and inspires me to write everyday. Love you, Joy.

To my friend and sister, Nadjia Ellis, thank you for all of your love and support. I love you.

To my God-daughter Anadia Clark and my God-son Jaheim Taylor, I appreciate you both so much. You two are jewels to me and your God-mommy loves you.

To the greatest church on this earth, New Life, and all of my spiritual sons and daughters from state to state, I thank each of you. You have inspired me in ways that words could never express. Your week to week anticipation and expectation you show, each of you pulled this relevation out of me. I love and appreciate all of you!!!!

"Your destiny is chosen by God. Your future is
certain. Whether you arrive there is up to you."
—Myles Munroe

TABLE OF CONTENTS

HAVE YOU EVER ASKED YOURSELF, "WHY DID GOD create me? What did He create me to do?" Perhaps, you've discovered the answers to those questions, but you just can't seem to to wrap your mind around the enormity of what God called you to do. You may be asking like David did, "Who am I, God, that you are mindful of me?" You may be wondering, "God, why did you create me for such an amazing task?" You may be thinking that God placed you in the wrong family—that you were raised on the wrong side of the tracks, and therefore, you're not cut out to perform the task He designed for you to complete. Perhaps, you are looking at your situation and noticing that you lack the resources needed to perform the task God has called you to, and you're trying to figure out how you're going to do what God called you to do. Maybe you don't even know where to start regarding the task God has given you. You have no help. No one to turn to. No clue. All you have is a dream, a vision God told you to write out. Perhaps, God may have shown you such great visions and plans because He is getting ready to use you to help someone else close to you carry out their assignment in life. God placed within you that which they so desperately need. Have you ever been told that you are too small to carry such a big dream? Maybe you've never been told any of the above. Perhaps, this one fits you: Have you ever been told that you will never become great in life or successfully complete anything in life due to your past failures? Or has your family who you expect to be your greatest support system ever doubted you and told you that you would never accomplish anything great in life? If you answered yes to any of the questions above, then this book is for you. The Holy Spirit inspired me to write this book to empower, educate, and strengthen "chosen vessels" like yourself—yes, you are God's chosen vessel. This book is designed to help you find your way and both discover and accomplish God's assignment for your life.

The questions above are questions I once asked myself. The statements above are statements made towards me. I was the one who was told that I could never be anything great, accomplish anything great because of my past failures; I was the one who was doubted by family members; I was the one questioning whether or not God placed me in the right family, whether or not I could accomplish God's will because of a lack of resources and support, and trying to figure my way through. I was facing the very same dilemma you're probably facing right now. But God provided for me clarity in this matter; and now, I am on assignment to provide clarity in your life. I am honored to be God's chosen vessel which He is using to speak to a chosen generation of Believers who've been selected by God to do a great work in the earth for the Lord in this season. Get ready! This is your season.

CHAPTER 1

CHOSEN

"Many are called, but few are chosen"
—Matthew 22:14

YOU WERE CREATED BY GOD TO ACCOMPLISH THE TASK God has predestined for you to accomplish. You are not here by accident. You are not a mistake. So don't be afraid of what others may think about you. God has anointed you to accomplish His will. You were born for this! You are already equipped with all that you need to accomplish what God has called you to do. You already have it! You were born with it! You have what it takes to be successful and to win! The Bible says, "Many are called, but few are chosen" (Matthew 22:14). When most people read this scripture they think it is saying God picks "certain" people to be great while overlooking others. That's not what this scripture is saying. This verse has often been taken out of content. This verse isn't saying God chooses some people to do His will and then overlook or ignore others when looking at the full parable in which it is contained. According to the parable here, Jesus said everyone is invited by God to partake of that which He has prepared and has been given the opportunity to adequately respond to God's invitation, but the ones who are "chosen" are the ones who responded to God's invitation. Therefore, this verse is simply telling us that we must respond to God's calling and be willing to walk in His power in order to fulfill the purpose He has for our lives. When you say yes to God, you place yourself in the category of "the chosen ones".

This parable explains the process by which we are called by God and chosen by Him. Let's take a deeper look at it. First, let's focus on the words "many" and "few". It is very easy to misunderstand the meaning of the word "many" in the New Testament because it has a slightly different meaning in the Greek language. In both languages, "many" refers to a large group, but in the English it is restrictive as opposed to the Greek where it is inclusive. In other words, if I say, "Many people came" in English, I am also emphasizing that many people did not come as well; however, in the Greek, this phrase ("Many people came") more-so implies that everyone did come—it doesn't focus on those who were restricted or didn't show up.

In this parable, everyone was invited to the wedding, but the invitation went out in two waves. The respectable people were invited first, but they did not heed the invitation. They lied about their reasons for not being able to attend the wedding banquet or pretended to be too busy with other things to attend; this resulting in the fact that none of these guests showed up. The king, therefore, instructed his servants to send out invitations once more, but this time they were to be given to individuals that were not on the original invitation list—they were to be given to "everyone" else, to any and all who would receive the invitation. And these people did show up. The major points to take away here are:

1. God chooses who He pleases. (In chapter two, I will expound more on this more.)
2. God has called everyone, but only those who receive the invitation are declared "chosen". (Again, I'll expound more on this in Chapter three.)
3. God has called each of us to fulfill an assignment on this earth, but if we choose not to do what He has called us to do, He will find a replacement for us as He did with the first group of invited guests in the parable. In essence, we can be replaced due to disobedience and hard-headedness.

As you read through this book, God is going to begin to give you clarity on why He chose you and on how to begin to walk in the things He has chosen for you to walk in, but it was important that we establish an understanding first of what it means to be "chosen" so that we'll possess the right mindset. Now that we understand the process of being chosen by God, let's explore more about this subject matter.

All throughout the Bible we find many "chosen" vessels (individuals) whose lives and actions we can examine and learn from. One example we can look at is Noah. The Bible says,

> "So God said to Noah, 'I am going to put an end to all people, for the earth is filled with violence because of them. I am surely going to destroy both them and the earth. So make yourself an ark of cypress wood; make rooms in it and coat it with pitch inside out.'"—Genesis 6:13-15

Noah was chosen by God to complete a critical task in the earth. We are God's workmanship in the earth, so when He tells us to do something, it's important to remember that these assignments may be time sensitive, therefore, we don't have time to waist questioning God; we just need to get up, take His word for it, and move on His instructions.

Although it may seem rather harsh and unseemly for such a just God to flood the earth with water as a form of judgment against mankind, without hesitation Noah obeyed GOD and began construction on the ark God instructed him to build. This story is one of the most important in the Old Testament because of what it communicates to us about God and the importance of obeying His instructions. Here are a couple of key points to take away from this passage of Scripture:

- It reveals to us that God is a holy God and that He cannot tolerate sin.
- It reveals to us that God is just and that no sin will go unpunished.
- It reveals to us that God is a God of mercy, being that

He spared some.

- It reveals to us the seriousness of God's judgment—the great deluge was worldwide and cataclysmic, demonstrating God's great power.

The Bible declares that Noah did everything God commanded him to do just as God commanded him to do it in Genesis 6:22. Noah followed God's strict orders immediately began building the Ark, which wasn't an easy task. Likewise, the things that God has instructs us to do might not be easy either. But I am sure that if Noah was here today, he would testify that the task God gave him wasn't easy, but it was worth it. Everything he endured during the process of carrying out God's command was certainly worth enduring in the end.

When I think about Noah, I often wonder about what thoughts might have been running through his mind while building the Ark. Did he get stressed out? Frustrated? Wonder why God gave him such a task? I'm sure Noah had all kind of thoughts running through his mind, even doubts and fears; furthermore, the Bible doesn't indicate that he confided in anyone during this process. Perhaps, he felt as if he couldn't confide in anyone. Who would believe him anyway? What ridicule would he subject himself to by sharing with others what God shared with him. Noah was human just like you and me. He was all alone in this process. And yet, he got up and did everything God instructed him to do without hesitation.

Why is it that when God speaks to us today, we feel like we need someone else to come behind Him to approve or validate what He spoke into our spirits? Instead of following after Noah's example, we do the opposite and wait for people to say, "Oh yeah, that's good. Do that." Sadly, today, more people are focused on putting man's word above God's word; we tend to obey man over God. But I can understand why we tend to do this because this was me a few years ago. While pastoring a church, God begin to speak to me more about my assignment on the earth; and while He was revealing my assignment to me, I grew frustrated due to the enormity of the vision He gave me concerning my life and calling. When God spoke to me about what He wanted me to do I was just a single parent raising four children. I didn't have much. I had just gone through a divorce and I was in a crazy place mentally and physically and was unsure about my life and future. I was also unsure about my future in the ministry. I was even unsure about God! I battled mentally with the reality of the divorce, questioning why God would allow it to occur after all of the praying and fasting I did. I pleaded with God earnestly to turn my marriage situation around and help me and my husband stay together, especially for the sake of our four kids, but that didn't happen, but He didn't grant me my request. I have to be honest with you here and admit that since, as I believed then, God didn't care to honor my request to keep my marriage together, I didn't want anything to do with Him…which also meant not wanting to serve Him in the ministry. I was in such a low place, feeling embarrassed and humiliated publicly in front of my church due to my divorce and feeling fearful due to the future of my home. It was in a hard place in life. I really didn't have any friends around to help me, to encourage me to remain hopeful in God and focus on the mighty things He was going to do in my life. But it was during this season that God began to speak to me about His mighty plan for my life. He began giving me visions of where He was taking me and what He was about to do in and through me. While receiving these revelations from God, I began to say in my heart, "God, stop!!! Please stop!!! There is absolutely no way I can accomplish these things! First of all, I don't even have a husband, someone to support me. How can I do these things with out a husband?!" I remember telling God that there was absolutely no way that I could plant all of the churches he was calling me to plant in all of the different states He was calling me to plant them without any help. I tried hard to argue my way out of my purpose. I came up with every excuse imaginable. But nothing I said worked. God kept on downloading revelations into my spirit throughout the day everyday concerning His will for me.

God is strategic. He knows how and when to perform a work in you. God picked the right time in my life to speak to me concerning His will. I was broken. I had nowhere else to turn and no one else to turn to. Without realizing it then, being in a hard place was where God wanted me to be so that He could speak to me. It was a good place for me. I know that sounds strange, but it's true. You see, it was in those moments that I began to pull on God like never before. Since I had nothing and no one to turn to for strength and guidance, I found myself turning to God more than ever before and drawing close to Him like never before. God knows what He's doing.

During this season in my life I began to hunger and thirst after God like never before. I began to understand this one important principle for the first time in my life: In order to become the person that God predestined for me to be and accomplish all that He predestined for me to accomplish, I had to become one with God on another lever. I couldn't remain at the same level in God where I was at and experience a higher level of His glory and blessings. I had to go higher in Him.

With that being said, it was through this process that God was taking me through that I became a true intercessor. I dived wholeheartedly into a life of prayer. I found prayer to be a place of comfort for me. Prayer became a necessity in my life, some I couldn't live without. I began to build my life around prayer. I built a prayer room in my home and even at my place of work. The time that I spent with God in prayer gave me life again.

Jesus declared in John 10;10 (NIV), "The thief's purpose is to steal, kill and destroy. My purpose is to give them a rich and satisfying life." Jesus' promise of abundant life here reminds me of other promises of God made to us like the ones found in Ezekiel 34:12-15, 25-31 and John 5:26.

So there I was, lying in my bed when God spoke to me as clear as day about building twelve ministries in several different states. I was like, "God, I already feel like I don't have spiritual guidance. I'm already feeling like I'm on an island all by myself. And now, you want me to do what?!!" I said, "Lord, I don't even have anyone to help me understand this pastoring thing, and now you're talking to me about building twelve different ministries in different states?! Really?!!" I also remember telling God, "God, you are so awesome! But whoever this vision is for, allow me to meet them and I promise You I will help them carry it out with out hesitation." God then said to me,

"I will equipped you, woman of God, to carry it out."

Before I said yes to God, I spent a lot of time crying and asking Him Why me? I believe that's one of the signs that you are chosen by God for something: you know within yourself that you wouldn't have selected the assignment God is calling you to carry out because there is absolutely no way that you could accomplish it in your own strength and ability. When God speaks to you about something that requires His strength and ability to accomplish in your life, you know it's Him speaking. He always puts us in the position to rely on Him to accomplish His will for our lives. His tasks for us are just that big, just that huge.

When I said to God, "Yes, I will go," it was official. And as I later discovered through experience, God has everything in place for us to complete our assignments when we step out on faith and in obedience to Him. You just have to say, "Lord, I will obey!" And when you do this, everything will begin to unfold immediately. Our obedience is truly better than anything else. For, as the Bible declares in 1 Samuel 15:22, "To obey is better than sacrifice, and to heed is better than the fat of rams." As Edwin Lois Cole, founder of the Christian Men's Network, an American religious organization devoted to helping Christian men and fathers, once stated, "A ton of prayer will never produce what an ounce of obedience will." Your obedience is crucial; it is critical in this hour. We are living in the End Days and Christ is soon to return; therefore, there is so much that God must accomplish in the earth before Jesus returns. Everything that God does in the earth He does through His creation: man. We are God's creation! He created you on purpose for a purpose! So allow Him to finish what He started in your life. You were chosen for this moment, for a purpose, for a might task. You were chosen for this!

CHAPTER 2

YOU ARE GOD'S CHOICE

"And they prayed and said, "Thou Lord, which knowest the heart of all men, show whether of these two thou hast chosen, that he may take part in this ministry and apostleship, from which Judas by transgression fell, that he might go to his own place. And they gave forth their lots: and the lot fell upon Matthias; and he was numbered with the eleven apostles."
—Acts 1:24-26

YOU ARE GOD'S CHOICE! THE SOONER YOU BEGIN TO accept this revelation, the sooner things around you will begin to change for your good and you will better understand everything that has transpired in your life as well as ascertain the things that have been difficult to comprehend in your life. Now, say this with me: I AM GOD'S CHOICE!!! You and I were chosen by God to do great things in the earth. We must always remember that we did not choose ourselves and neither were we chosen by man. Since our callings come from God, it is important that we stay in God presence, pursuing His face. Who God chooses, He is obligated to equip for the task given, and He is obligated to provide the strategy needed to accomplish the task. God wouldn't be fair if He didn't provide these things. That's just one of the things that makes God so awesome!

When the eleven disciples prayed and asked God who was to be chosen to replace Judas Iscariot, the disciple who committed suicide after hanging himself, God chose a man named Matthias. The disciples didn't choose Matthias; God did. Scripture does not explain why God chose Matthias over Joseph. The other eleven disciples didn't question God's decision either; they just openly welcomed God's chosen man onto the team and continued doing the work that God gave them to do. God knows what He has placed on the inside of us.

Matthias' (whose name in the Hebrew is translated *Mattityahu*) calling as an apostle is unique in that his appointment was not made by Jesus who had already ascended into heaven, and his appointment was also made before the Holy Spirit's descent upon the early church. It's interesting that there is no mention of anyone named Matthias in any of the Synoptic Gospels; but according to the Book of Acts, this man had been with Jesus from His baptism by John the Baptist until His resurrection and ascension into heaven. Other than that, there is no further information found on Matthias in the Canonical New Testament. The only thing we know about this man is… he was chosen by God.

There is a specific task God has anointed you for in this earth. Like I mentioned at the beginning of the book, there is no need to be afraid of failing at your assignment in life because you were designed specifically for just that— you are anointed for it. It fits you perfectly. Don't worry about what it's going to take to complete the assignment nor how you will complete it. You will. You were created to. God is going to supply you with everything you need in order that you may accomplish that which He called you to accomplish in the earth. So lean totally on God in this season. He will not fail you. He will guide you every step of the way. The Bible says, "Trust in the Lord with all your heart and do not lean on your own understanding. In all your ways acknowledge him and he will make your path straight" (Proverbs 3:5-6).

Since Matthias was hand-picked by God as Judas' replacement, it was God's responsibility to equip Matthias for the work that he was about to partake in. God is a fair God. He will never call you and not equip you. He won't call you and not provide the anointing you need to walk in the task He called you to accomplish. Likewise, God would never call you and not send the right people around you to help you accomplish your task. Notice that God chose Matthias and then began training him for the role and assignment on his life using the other disciples. And not only that, but Matthias also had the guidance of the Holy Spirit in his life. God set him up for success.

Matthias wasn't worried about what others thought

about him as an apostle. He simply focused on doing what God instructed him to do. We must learn from Matthias' example. He spent less time worrying about who would or wouldn't accept his nomination as an apostle by God and more time focusing on walking in his calling. This is the attitude all of us must learn to take on if we're going to fulfill our divine destinies.

One of the greatest distractions we face as vessels of God is fear: fear of what others might think, fear of what others might do, fear of failure, etc. There are too many gifted and anointed people today who are sitting back spending an enormous amount of time living in the cave of fear, scared to come out and do what God has called them to do. You can't be that way! You can't! We only have only a short amount of time to fulfill our assignments on the earth; therefore, it is essential that we use our time wisely, not waste it foolishly. Don't use the little amount of time you have on this earth hiding and cowering in the cave of fear as if God didn't choose you for an assignment and can't see you through it. Again, God chose…YOU! When God created you, He did so for a purpose, an amazing one. As He stated in Jeremiah 1:5 when speaking to the young prophet, Jeremiah, "Before I formed you in the womb I Knew you. Before you were born I set you apart; I appointed you as a prophet to the nations." This is one of my most favorite scriptures. As a chosen vessel of God's in the earth, remember those words which God spoke to Jeremiah and know that they also apply to your life today. Notice there that God explained to Jeremiah that He knew him even before he was in his mother's womb. Yes, I said it: Before the womb! Catch what God is saying here in this passage of scripture: You and I were on God's mind before we were even conceived, and our purposes were already established before our conceptions. God didn't try to figure out what to do with you after you were born; He custom-made you for a certain task before you were even conceived. You came ready-made. He shaped you for it. Nothing about you is an accident. Nothing. We're not simply the byproduct of a night of pleasure between some man and some woman. No! You are the brainchild of God Himself! You were first conceived in the mind of God before being conceived in the earth. You came from greatness for greatness. It's not your parents who brought you into existence; it was God. It's not your parents who can usher you into your greatness; only God can. God needs you to understand that you were created by Him and for His purpose.

That verse in Jeremiah goes even deeper than that. In Jeremiah, God also said that He set Jeremiah apart from everyone else. Think about that. God set you apart from everyone else! This means you were created to be different. Said another way: You weren't created to fit in. You were designed to be peculiar. So stop feeling bad about not fitting in. That's not what God designed you to do.

You are meant to be who God created you to be. What you were created to be and what you were created to do is all tied up in God. You discover these things in God, not people. God will finish what He started in you…if you allow Him to. Although everyone on the earth was created by God for a purpose, many will miss their purposes due to their refusal to allow God to guide them. They want to do great things without God. They don't want to submit to His guidance, His counsel, and His power. That's where many miss it! They try to be great and do great things in their own power and strength, using their own intellect.

Another thing God told Jeremiah was that he was anointed to be a prophet to the nations. God knows us before our conception and birth and He loved each and everyone of us in a very special way, not only calling unto Himself in a state of holiness, but also separating us for Himself alone so that we may walk in the offices He predetermined for us before the world began just as He did the Apostle Paul—separating him to Himself for the evangelistic work of ministry in the earth. As Paul acknowledged himself, "Paul, a servant of Christ Jesus, called to be as Apostle and set apart for the Gospel of God" (Romans 1:1). Do you know who you are? Do you know whose you are? Do you know you were called by God before you were even born? God knows you. He knows those who are His and has chosen for eternal life not only before their formation in their mothers' wombs, but before the foundation of the world. I like the way the psalmist puts it in Psalms 139:15-16:

> "My frame was not hid from thee, when I was made in secret, and curiously wrought in the lowest parts of the earth. Thine eyes did see my substance, yet being imperfect: and in thy book all my members were written, which in continuance were fashioned, when as yet there was none of them."

The phrase "lowest parts of the earth" is usually associated with death (Psalm 63:9; Ezekiel 26:20), but here it refers to the concealment of the womb. The concept of the Lord's "book" where it is recorded all of our "members" reinforces the idea of God's sovereign power over life and death. Every part of you was fashioned by God.

When you read Psalms 139: 7-16, keep in mind that although we cannot see God, He can see us. God sees everything about us, including all that we do and say. The psalmist couldn't venture outside of the Lord's sight. "Whither can I go?" the psalmist asked. From the furthermost corners of the globe—even in heaven and hell—he couldn't go beyond God's reach. No veil can hide us from God. No. Not even the thickest of darkness. No disguise can mask our true conditions, our true motives, from God's sight.

Dearly beloved, I want you understand if nothing else that God sees everything you do and He knows everything about you. Everything! And only He knows what you were created to do, what you desire to do, and what you will do. God knows all! He knew everything about you before you even existed on this earth. You don't possess any weaknesses or shortcomings that God doesn't already know about. You don't even possess and challenges and obstacles that God isn't aware of. He knows...EVERYTHING about you. And yet, in spite of all of your shortcomings and obstacles, God chose you for a major work in this earth. So stop being afraid and simply walk in that which you were called by God to walk in and be who God called you to be. No more fear! Walk by faith! You are who you are for a reason!! You were chosen for the task you were selected for for a reason!

I decree and declare today that you are coming out of that cave you've been living in now! Your cave days are over!! You days of hiding have come to an end!!

God had you on His mind before anything else. He breathed into your nostrils life and a purpose. When God was creating you, He held the blueprint for your life in the palm of His hand. He already had a plan for your life. You have be chosen, selected, for a great plan in this earth. God's plans supersedes any plans we can come up with on our own. And it is for this reason that I want to make sure that you understand how significant you are, how anointed you are…and why you are anointed.

CHAPTER 3

OVERCOMING YOUR PAST

"But the Lord said to Ananias, 'Go! This man is my chosen instrument to proclaim my name to the Gentiles and their kings and to the people of Israel.'"
—ACTS 9:15

I can hear you saying now, "God, what about the things I did? I know I don't deserve to be used by you!" To that, God is saying,

"My daughter/My son, even these things will not make me change my mind about you. You were chosen for this!"

Beloved, yes you messed up. Yes, you did things you are not proud of. Yes, it the things you have done were shameful and unbecoming of you. Some of the people you hurt will continue to be upset with you, maybe even un-forgiving towards you. Some of them may be hesitant and reluctant to ever trust you again. You might not ever fall back into favor with some of the people you've wronged. Although you've gone through so many changes in your life, there will be some who will never believe you have changed. Some have written you off as incorrigible, as ir-redeemable; and they will never downplay your past nor fail to remind you of it so as long as you shall live. But you must move forward. You have a bright future ahead of you in Christ. God has work for you to do. There's too much to be done for you to remain stuck in the past. You've done what is necessary to right the wrongs you've done to others, now it is time for you to focus on the work ahead of you.

If you're going to accomplish the task God set be-fore you, you must get out of that pit of pity, regret, and shame. GET UP!!! You're still alive! You still have warm blood flowing through your veins! You still have a purpose! You still have work to do! Whatever you went through didn't kill you! Whatever you did, God has forgiven you for it! Realize that there is more to you than your mistakes and your failures. Great people fall everyday; they fail and make mistakes just like you; but what makes them great is the fact that they always get back up and jump back into the race. The Bible says in Ecclesiastes 9:1, "The race is not given to the swift, nor the battle to the strong…"

God has His hand on your life even before you told that lie, committed adultery, fornicated with that man/woman, stole that money, said all of those mean things to your love ones, committed that crime, committed that murder, engaged in or experienced that rape, etc. There is no sin Jesus didn't die for on the cross. Moses was a murderer, and yet, even he found grace. Abraham was a lier, and yet, he found grace. David was an adulterer and a murderer who took another man's wife, and yet, even he found grace after confessing his sins. You are no different, nor are you beyond God's reach. But you must know this: Before you did whatever it is that you did, God called you and equipped you for a mighty purpose in the earth. God is still calling your name!

I wish I can say I was/am perfect, but I can't. I made many mistakes—so many mistakes. But not even my mess was able to get God to change his mind about me. Absolutely nothing that you have experienced or is experiencing will make God change his mind about you because of His unconditional love towards you. When He called you, He knew what He was doing. God did not make a mistake by choosing you. You may think God made a mistake. Others may think God made a mistake. But He didn't. I am a living testimony to this. Despite how much I messed up and went astray, doing things according to my fleshly desires, God always had a way of escape in place for me. God knew how to put the right people in my path to say the right things and help me to get back on track with His original plan for my life.

Sometimes, I wonder why God didn't just let me go; why He didn't just let me die. I should have died so many times and be resting in my grave today, but God stopped death from taking me and destroyed the works of the enemy (Satan) in my life. Actually, I should be in prison, but God… God knows I've made too many of the wrong decisions in my life, decisions that caused my-self and my family much heartache, headache, and pain. God has delivered me time and time again from the consequences of my own actions. I would ask God the question, "God, what about what I did?" Actually, I asked God this very question for days, weeks, months. I just couldn't wrap my mind around the fact that a God that is so holy and mighty would still want to use someone like me. So many times before when God would call my name, I wasn't trying to submit to His will. I was still looking for love in all of the wrong places and trying to be my own god. And then when I did finally say yes to God, my next excuse was this: "God, no one is going to want to hear anything from me and my *jacked-up* self. So, God you have to find someone else to carry this task. I am not fit to preach or teach to anyone!" Once, I even told God that I would screw up His entire Kingdom agenda because "I'm nothing but a screw-up!" I boldly told God He was wasting His anointing on me. I felt it necessary to "inform" God of all of my short-comings and of the reasons why I was a bad candidate for His will…as if He didn't already know these things.

One day, while telling God all of these things, He simply whispered in my spirit to get up, grab my Bible, and read Acts the ninth chapter in its entirety. I immediately obeyed His voice. To be honest, I was hoping that He was sending me to the scriptures to tell me what I wanted to hear, which was that He couldn't use me because I had too many issues. But that's not what He told me. Instead, He amplified His voice through Acts the ninth chapter. Allow me to share with you what the Holy Spirit shared with me in this passage of Scripture:

Imagine for a moment that Saul has just arrived at Damascus. By this time, Saul has gained a reputation as the ringleader of a movement to make Christianity extinct. A devout Hellenistic Jew from the tribe of Benjamin who was born in Tarsus of Cilicia, Saul was a member of the Pharisees and was taught by none other than Gamaliel who we met in Acts 5;34-40. Saul did not agree with his teacher, Gamaliel, on how Christians should be dealt with. Saul's solution for dealing with the problem of Christians was to arrest, try, convict, and punish them with imprisonment and even death. Saul's career as a persecutor of Christians seemed to begin with a man named Stephen, who was appointed as a deacon in the early church. After disposing of Stephen in brutal fashion, Saul's reputation spread quickly throughout the land and especially throughout the Christian community in Jerusalem (Acts 7;58-8-3). And after killing Stephen, Saul's thirst for blood increased as he would not be content until he had driven every Christian in existence out of the holy city (Jerusalem). After persecuting Christians in Jerusalem, Saul's appetite for blood grew as he decided to extend his reach beyond the holy city—he now wanted to drive every Christian off of the face of the earth regardless of where they were found. So Saul decided to start going to other looking for (or rather hunting after) Christians to arrest and take back to Jerusalem for punishment. One of the towns Saul decided to visit was a city called Damascus, which was 150 miles northeast of Jerusalem. In Damascus, word got out that Saul was coming. There was panic among Believers there. Imagine if you will that you were a Christian who had just arrived in Damascus and you learned of the whereabouts of a group of Believers. You go to be a part of the worship experience with these likeminded Believers; and upon arrival, you notice that everyone has gathered together in a sense of urgency for a time of prayer after being informed of Saul's coming—Saul was on his way with legal authorization from the Chief Priest and the Sanhedrin to arrest and extradite the saints who were in the city. Let me ask you this question: What do you think the saints in that town might have been praying for? Well I believe their Prayer would have been? Of course! "Lord, please save us from Saul!!!"

When I read Acts the ninth chapter, I found myself crying because I couldn't wrap my mind around how a person could be so cruel and filled with so much hatred of Christians and how God could be so loving towards such an individual. While reading this chapter, the Holy Spirit said to me, "And even this wouldn't have made Me change My mind about him (Saul)."

After the Holy Spirit told me that, I began to cry even harder, wondering how God could even trust someone like that. The more I asked Him, the more He replied, "Even this wouldn't make Me change My mind about his original purpose in the earth."

Afterwards, I began to read a little bit further in this chapter. I read how as Saul journeyed towards Damascus, suddenly there "shined round about him a light from heaven; and he fell to the earth, and heard a voice saying unto him, Saul, Saul, why persecutest thou Me?" (Acts 9:3-4)

Everything we have done and will do God is aware of; and yes, He will deal with us according to our actions. Don't get me wrong. God will chastise us. Sometimes very painfully. But God knows all of these things about us and still chooses us.

After the light shined from heaven, Saul was immediately knocked off of his horse and onto the ground. God then asked Saul, "Why persecutest thou Me?" There is something about the voice of God when you are in a very low place. God's voice is amplified through our suffering. The Scripture places emphasis on Saul being on the ground when God spoke to him. That speaks volumes! You might be in one of the lowest places in your life right now, but know that you are in a good place—you are in a place where God can speak to you. Never devalue your low places. Never underestimate the places God has allowed you to end up in. Never underestimate a good fall. My fall was good for me. It was through my fall that God was able to finally get my attention.

Later on in the text, Saul responded to God, asking, "Who art thou, Lord?" I find it interesting that at this point Saul calls Jesus "Lord." I doubt that Saul recognized the voice speaking to him as that of Jesus'. Saul's use of the title "Lord" was most likely honorific, being equivalent to saying "Sir". I can't say that Saul knew whose voice he was hearing—that he knew it was the divine voice of the Messiah, the Savior, Jesus the Christ. Nonetheless, Acts 9:6 states that with great trembling and astonishment,

Saul asked God, "What will you have me to do?" Think about that: The big, bad Saul who was such a force to be reckoned with is now on the ground begging for God to reveal His will to him. Saul is not only on the ground at this point; he is also physically blind due to the intensity of the light he was exposed to.

God took Saul (whose name He later changed to Paul) through a process, a deliverance process. This is why God can still perform a mighty work in and through you. Once God delivers you and anoints you after your fall, you will be brand new. You won't look like nor feel like that which God delivered you from.

Your mistakes did not catch God by surprise. Your mess-ups did not catch God off guard. God still insists on using you for His glory. He has great plans for you. God forgave and delivered Saul and then changed his name. Likewise, He desires to deliver you and give you a new name. Your new name is Victory! You will be victorious! You will give birth to the greatness lying on the inside of your belly!

Acts 9:13-15 says,

"Then Ananias answered, Lord I have heard by many of this man, how much evil he hath done to thy saints at Jerusalem: And here he hath authority from the chief priest to bind all that call on thy name. But the Lord said unto him, Go thy way: for he is a chosen vessel unto me, to bear my name before the Gentiles and kings and the children of Israel…"

Nothing in your past will make God change His mind about what He created you to do in the earth realm. Ananias thought God was crazy for choosing someone like Saul. Some people may say the same thing about you: that God is crazy for selecting you. But it doesn't matter what others think or say. You were chosen.

When I read Acts the ninth chapter, it was then and only then that began to believe God when he told me that my past didn't exclude me from His mighty plan in the earth. My past didn't stop Him from pursuing me so that He could do a mighty work in and through me for His glory. I was finally convinced that my mistakes in life didn't change God's mind about using me.

Shake off that guilt! Kick loose from that shame and get to moving towards your destiny and your purpose! Remember Paul as you journey along the way towards greatness. If God forgave someone like Paul even used him mightily, then He will surely use you. God gets joy out of cleaning us up and using us for His glory.

1 John 1:9 says, "If we confess our sins, He is faithful and just and will forgive us our sins and purify us from all unrighteousness." All we have to do is confess our sins and activate our faith and believe that our loving God will forgive us. The verse also says that God will purify us from all unrighteousness. This means God will cleanse us from our pasts and iniquities, leaving no residue. So never allow Satan to hold you hostage in your mind, causing you to believe his false report. Satan's report claims God will never forgive you for your mistakes. Don't believe that! 2 Corinthians 5:17 declares, "Therefore, if anyone is in Christ, he is a new creation. Old things have passed away,

and behold, all things have been made new." We are made new when surrender our lives to God. Walk in your newness. You are no longer the same person you once were when you're in Christ. Allow God to come in and change you and clean you up.

I love my newness! Choosing to walk with Jesus was the best decision I could have ever made in my life! He loves me and I love Him! And He loves you too, chosen one!

CHAPTER 4

ALL FOR YOUR GOOD

"You intended to harm me, but God intended it for good to accomplish what is now being done, the saving of many lives."—Genesis 50:20 NIV

EVERYTHING THAT SATAN TRIED TO SET UP IN MY LIFE from day one to destroy me didn't work. And not only did Satan's plans not succeed, but God used them for my good. When you submit wholeheartedly to God, you will certainly accomplish everything that He has predestined for you to accomplish. Every assignment and invention that has been locked up on the inside of you for years will come forth. I want you to get into position because you are about to give birth to your purpose.

I was born and raised in a small town called Clewiston, Florida. My hometown was such a loving city then just as it is today. The city was filled with individuals that cared about one another and practically shared everything with each other. If a family went lacking, it was hard to tell since everyone helped everyone. I have so many great memories of that town.

My beautiful mother, Vernie Lee Allen, was my heart. She was the heartbeat of our family. I observed how she loved and took care of her mother and siblings. She was absolutely amazing. Although we lived in the projects—we didn't have a car, fancy clothes, expensive shoes, and hardly any food—I wouldn't trade that experience growing up with anything.

My mother was a strong African American single parent, but she was a drug addict. She had to have drugs before when she went bed at night and had to have them the moment she woke up in the morning. Drugs gave momma something I could never understand; they made her feel like her world was coming together when it really falling apart. I gave her love, tried to be a good girl, and worked hard in school to get good grades because I thought these things would make her want to get off of drugs, but nothing I did would motivate her to stop using.

I would keep the house clean. I'd cook and take care of the other kids in order to take the load off of my mom so she wouldn't get too stressed out. I wanted her to feel comfortable and relaxed at home, hoping that that would keep her out of the streets. Anything that could be done to keep my mother away from drugs, I was willing to do. But sadly, drugs completely dominated my mother's life.

I can recall one Thanksgiving morning waking up and noticing that my mother had been out all night long. My siblings and I would be hungry soon and the Thanksgiving food was still in the refrigerator ready to be cooked—but someone had to cook it. So I got up and begin cooking Thanksgiving dinner that day. Suddenly, my mom arrived home. When she came through the door, she could smell the aroma. I had the turkey in the oven and the rest of the meal was almost done. My entire family remembers that incident. My mother just screamed at the top of her lungs, "This girl done cooked all my food!!!" For several days she was hot with me, but she also said she was proud of me for doing what I did. At the time, I was only 11yrs old. That day, she told me that one day I was going to be a great mom and a great cook. That word "great" stood out to me. To be told that I was going to be great at something was reassuring. But God had a great plan for my life and was using even the struggles in my household back then to shape me into a woman of destiny and purpose.

I would cook and clean and take care of the house while my mom would spend much of her time in the streets looking for drugs. Over time, she grew worse. Seemingly, nothing could stop her addiction. It looked like the more I did to take her mind off of the streets, the more she wanted the streets.

Eventually, due to her activities in the streets, my mother ended up being diagnosed with AIDS. As a child, this news confused me. This occurred in 1986 during a time when there wasn't a lot of information available about AIDS. There was such a stigma around the disease due to society's ignorance of it. At the time, people actually believed that the disease was transferable through touching. So, because of my mother's sickness many people would treat me and my siblings differently. I lost many friends because of my mother's sickness, even boyfriends. Still, God had a plan for my life.

My mother's sickness made me angry and bitter. I was willing to fight anyone anywhere due to the anger inside of me. I felt betrayed by God because of my mother's situation. Between the drugs and AIDS, I really can't say which one damaged my mother the most.

Despite all of her shortcomings, my mother was an amazing woman who loved her children with a love that's unexplainable. And although she struggled with so many things in her life, she truly loved God. She loved to sing gospel music.

In 1988, my mother died. This left a whole in my heart. My mom was my inspiration, my cheerleader; she was my everything. Behind her death, I grew even angrier towards God. I decided to stop believing in Him. I wanted my mom back. I would often ask God, "How could you allow a great woman to die like that? How could you do this to children that are already fatherless?" My dad and my siblings' fathers were around (my siblings and I had the same mother but different fathers), but they weren't involved in our lives. They weren't real fathers. My mother raised us all five of us by herself with the aid of her mother. They did the best they could.

During the time of my mother's sickness, I took care of her. I was a 12yr old taking care of a severely sick mother. I had to be home-schooled because of it. But I enjoyed every moment of taking care of my mom. I was the middle child. My oldest sister had primarily been raised by my grandmother and my big brother was in and out of jail, so the burden of responsibility for caring for our sick mom fell on me. But God even though the load was tough, God was using this situation to mold and shape my character.

As I stated a moment ago, I was very angry with God. I believed God was picking on me. I certainly didn't believe God had plans for my life. Although I loved taking care of my mother, I still felt as if I was being robbed of a childhood. While other girls my age were enjoying their lives, having fun and doing fun things, I was mainly confined to the house watching my mother die slowly. I felt like God selected me in life to demonstrate to everyone else what an embarrassment looked like. At first, I wanted to disbelieve in God, but eventually, my resentment towards Him morphed into hatred. I developed contempt in my heart for God. See, I knew quite a bit about God while young because my grandmother would make us go to Sunday School and church all of the time growing up. I remember in Sunday School class my teachers talking about how good God was. I was wondering where was this good God? I needed to meet Him because the one that I was seeing wasn't being fair. I was in a bad state of mind and had lost all hope of seeing a better day. I had absolutely no faith in God—in His plan to use me, in His love for me, in His ability to take the pain of my childhood and turn it into something that would serve a greater purpose in my life.

After my mother's death, my life began to go downhill. I began to drink, smoke, become very promiscuous, and do everything I thought I was big and bad enough to do. I was just lonely, lost, and hurting, now feeling fatherless and motherless. I then began to feel as if it was useless to live. So I wanted to commit suicide. On several occasions I sought to do so, but God would not allow it.

After I saw that I couldn't kill myself, I decided to give God another chance. In 1990, I rededicated my life to God. That was the best day of my life. I told God, "God, if you would just be my mother, I can get through this." And that's what He did. He was my mother and my father all in one. I begin to read his Word. I developed a love and a passion for studying His Word.

When you invite God into your life, immerse yourself in His Word, grow in the understanding and necessity of prayer, and develop a prayer life, your life will change immediately. My life did a complete 180 degree turn once I allowed the Holy Spirit to take control of my life and lead me. God had an awesome plan for my life, I just didn't understand this while going through the process I had to go through to become who God wanted me to be.

What God begin in me in 1990 was simply amazing. He began changing my surroundings, putting people in my life that were able and willing to teach me about Him. God moved me from my Hometown to Ft. Lauderdale, Florida with my aunt Bernice and uncle Calvin. They taught me how to love God and how to love myself. I know it was hard on them to make all of the sacrifices they made for me, but I'm grateful that they did.

By this time in my life, I had stop going to school

and had no desire to finish or do anything with my life. But my family strengthened me through the Word of God and helped me to understand the need to go back to school and get my diploma. By God's grace, I enrolled in night school and attended daytime classes at Dillard High School and then received my high school diploma.

The point I'm trying to make is it wasn't until I allowed the Holy Spirit into my life and allowed Him to lead and guide me that I began to understand my purpose and God's plan for my life and that I began to understand the purpose behind the pain I experienced growing up.

Oftentimes, I look back over my life and think to myself, The good in my life certainly does outweigh the bad. Although I encountered so many things as a child, I honestly can say that God caused all things in my life to work out for my good. All that I experienced made me the wife, mother, and pastor that I am today. Looking back now, I wouldn't trade my journey for anything. I'm grateful now that God took me the way that He did. For many years, I felt like Joseph in the Bible—like I had been picked out to be picked on. But, even still, deep down on the inside of me, even while going through all of the things I was going through and thinking all of the negative thoughts towards God that I was thinking, I have to honestly admit that I somehow knew that God was in the midst of my pain and suffering and that He had a plan to do something great in and through me.

Now that I have told you a little bit about me and revealed to you how my circumstances didn't make it appear as if God was in control of my life even though He was, let's take a look at another example from the Bible where God appeared to be absent during someone's pain but was actually there the whole time moving behind the scenes to execute His divine plan.

The Bible tells us in Genesis 37:1-5,

> "Jacob lived in the land where his father had stayed, the land of Canaan. This is the account of Jacobs family line. Joesph, a young man of seventeen, was tending the flocks with his brothers, the sons of Bilhah and the sons of Zilpah, his fathers wives, and he brought their father a bad report about them. Now Israel loved Joseph more than any of his other cons, because he had been born to him in his old age: and he made an ornate robe for him. When the brothers saw that their father loved him more than any of them, they hated him and could not speak a kind word to him. Joseph had a dream, and when he told it to his brothers, they hated him all the more." (NIV)

As always, God has a plan in every situation we encounter. In this text, God had a plan to bless Jacob's entire household, which He began to execute through Joseph, Jacob's son. Joseph, without realizing it, had been selected by God for a bigger purpose than what he previously imagined. God chose him to save his entire people from extinction. All of the hardship and pain Joseph endured prepared him for that purpose. I am sure that you have encountered many difficult and painful things in your life, but understand that it's all a part of God's awesome plan for your life! He is about to receive glory through it all. One of the most agonizing feelings one can experience is to feel isolated and rejected. I believe Satan attempts to get God's people all alone so that he can whisper lies into their ears and mislead them. When alone, Satan will often tell us things like these:

- You are alone
- Nobody loves you
- You are not worth anything
- You will never accomplish anything good in your life
- God doesn't love you

Of course, these are just a few of the lies Satan tells us and tries to convince us of in hopes of getting us to give up on God's plan for our lives, but you must understand that these are all lies and choose not to believe them. God has too much in store for your life for you to give up on Him and yourself because of the lies of the devil.

Notice in our text above that it was Joseph's own brothers—his own blood—who were trying to harm him, not strangers. And his brothers wanted to destroy his life all because of jealousy. These guys were jealous of their brother Joseph for a few reasons:

- Because Joseph was his father's favorite son
- Because Joseph's father had made and given him a special gift: a coat of many colors that symbolized favor
- Because God had given Joseph a startling dream of the future

Because of these things, ten of Joseph's brothers conspired against him and threw him into a pit while trying to figure out what to do with him. They actually sat down and ate dinner while their brother Joseph was crying out and pleading with them from the pit to spare his life and let him go. They were acting as if they had done nothing wrong—as if they didn't know their own blood brother was in that pit, begging and pleading for his life. After eating, they spotted a group of Ishmaelites from Gilead traveling through. Aha! We'll sell Joseph to them, they decided. That way they could permanently get rid of Joseph without having to kill him with their own hands. They would then come up with an excuse for Joseph's disappearance to tell their father.

I Know what you are thinking: How can one's own family be so cruel? How can blood brothers hate each other like this? How could life be so cruel to Joseph? But when you continue to read about the life of Joseph, you'll notice that Joseph was a dreamer—God would give him special dreams about the future; therefore, God knew before Joseph's brothers even threw him in a pit all of the things that Joseph was about to endure. The dream came before the pit. The dream came before the prison. And yes, the dream came before the palace.

Joseph was taken away from his beloved father as well as a beloved baby brother, Benjamin, who looked up to him and loved him dearly. Suddenly, Joseph found himself a stranger in a foreign land. Sometimes, on the road to purpose and destiny, you may find yourself being led by God to and through some strange places, places where you feel completely out of place and lost. But realize that

God is with you and that He will never leave you. Deuteronomy 31:6 says, "Be strong and Courageous. Do not be afraid or terrified because of them, for the Lord your God goes with you: He will never leave you nor forsake you."

You are not alone! The Holy spirt is ready to guide you into all truth as well as protect you from everything the enemy sends your way to stop you from accomplishing that which God called you to do. God has a plan for your life—an awesome plan! You are chosen!

CHAPTER 5

DISCOVERING YOUR PURPOSE

"The purpose of a person's heart are deep waters, but one who has insight draws them out."—Proverbs 20:5

EVERYONE WAS CREATED IN THE IMAGE OF GOD AND was created with a purpose in life, but whether or not we discover this purpose or miss it entirely is up to us. When we have the Holy Spirit in our lives, we gain insight into God's purposes for us. Only through God's Holy Spirit can we gain a sense the confidence and the inward confirmation that we are right where we belong in God's overall scheme of things. The Holy Spirit will also notify us when we aren't where we supposed to be.

It is vitally important that you discover your purpose on this earth. So many people in the world today have absolutely no clue what their purposes are, but you after you complete this chapter you will begin to discover your purpose if you haven't already.

I read a story once about a man who netted three big fish from a mountain stream and carefully placed them side-by-side onto a thick patch of grass. Before he removed them from the water, they were like a liquid ballet: graceful; vibrant; moving elegantly. But as those fish laid on the grass, they became motionless; their eyes were were transfixed as they gasped for air. They looked and acted a little stupid.

The man noticed that they seemed very unhappy, so he began to talk to them, hoping that his encouragement would change their attitudes. "Little fish, don't be sad. You'll like the grass. Just try it out for a while," he told them. Still, there was no movement and no response from them. No exhibited change. A few more seconds passed and the man's brother walked by. "Hey, Bro! Come and check out these fish!" he told his brother. The brother sauntered over and the man explained that he was certain the fish could adjust to life on the grass. "I'm sure they could prosper here on the grass. Don't you agree?" he said.

"Why not?" the brother replied. So he joined in also and began telling the fish that it would be good if they learned to like the grass. After all, he liked the grass, so why shouldn't they? Still, the fish didn't blink. They just laid there, looking dumber and dumber by the second.

Finally, another brother approached them and asked them, "What are you doing?! Put them back! They can't be all they've been created to be when they are out of the water!" Finally convinced, the man carefully placed each fish back into the water stream. After splashing for a split second, all three fish swam away effortlessly, looking again like a liquid ballet. What ease! What grace! What beauty!

In that moment, the main brother realized that no matter how long he kept the fish in the grass, they would have never adjusted to the grass, they would have never been satisfied. Even if the fish tried to convince themselves that they could learn to like the grass, they never would have adapted to the grass and prospered in it. In fact, they would eventually died.

Do you feel like a fish out of water? Do you feel like you are misplaced in this world? Your sense of dissatisfaction with where you are and your natural God-given gifts, passions, and tendencies as well as the voices of others may all be screaming at you, telling you that what you're doing is not what you were created to do and that you were created for another purpose. Just like those fish, you feel like you are dying inside. But this inner sense agony is just what you need to push you out of your comfort-zone and into your ocean of destiny—into the place of greatness God has called you to. You were created for something greater!

God works through all situations to fulfill his purpose in your life. For the Bible declares, "And we know that in all things God works for the good of those who love him, who have been called according to his purpose" (Romans 8:28).

When God was fashioning you, He gave you gifts (special abilities, special powers) that are suited specifically for your purpose in life. These things are what make unique and different from all other people. God made you unique. He knows what He has given you and why He has created you. Nehemiah 9:6 says,

> "You alone are the Lord. You have made the heavens, the heaven of heavens with all their host, the earth and all that is on it, the seas and all that is in them. You give life to all of them and the heavenly host bows down before You."

Wow! Nehemiah said "the earth and all that is on it" was made by God and belongs to God. We are a part of this earth; therefore, God made us and He knows everything about us. With this in mind, discovering your purpose shouldn't be hard because you know who holds your purpose in the palm of His hand. All you have to learn how to do is communicate with He who holds your purpose in His hand. "But how do I communicate with God?" you ask. Prayer. This is our way of communicating with God. "But what exactly is prayer? And what should we say to God when we pray?" you may be asking. All prayer through these phases: Tell, Ask, and Listen. Let me elaborate on these three phases:

- *Tell*: God already knows everything that you're experiencing, but He wants you to trust Him with your heart. Be honest about what you're going through, thinking about, and what you're feeling. Talk about what excites you and what disappoints you, what makes you happy and what makes you sad. Tell Him you love Him, you're thankful for Him, and you praise Him for who

He is and what He does.

- *Ask*: God wants us to ask Him for what we need because by depending on Him for our needs He can build our trust in Him. No matter how big or small the need is, it matters to God. We can ask God for help, strength, provision, and guidance. He told us, "Call on me and I will answer you. I'll tell you marvelous and wondrous things that you could never figure out on your own" (Jeremiah 33:3, MSG).

- *Listen*: Prayer is a conversation with God, and during a conversation, one person doesn't do all of the talking. Conversation is essential in the communication process, and communication is an important part of every healthy relationship, including and especially our relationship with God. The more time we spend with Him, getting to know Him and discovering His love for us, and learning to listen to Him as He speaks to us, the more He will begin to give us details about why He created us. The more time we spend with God, the more He confirms to us in various ways that we have been chosen by Him to complete an awesome task, a task that has been lying dormant on the inside of you.

Another important step in discovering your purpose is learning to listen to your heart's dissatisfaction and discontentment. Now of coarse, we've been taught that dissatisfaction is a bad thing and that we should do everything possible to avoid it and ignore it; that we should act like it doesn't bother us even though it does. Put on a smile, people say. Go and buy something new or decide that misery is just a part of "bearing your cross." Above all else, don't consider the possibility that God might be using your dissatisfaction and discontentment to make you uncomfortable so you'll want to jump into the water like the fish in our story earlier and dwell in the very place where your gifts can shine. The Bible does tell us that dissatisfaction can sometimes be a result of spiritual warfare (Ephesians 6:10-12), and not an indication that we are out of God's will. But, wait a minute! Dissatisfaction can also be a road sign alerting us to the fact that we're headed in the wrong direction in life and that God wants us to go in another direction: the direction of our purpose.

If you're miserable in your current career or job or whatever you may be involved in and you are dissatisfied (and you have been for a long time), then consider that God may be subtly steering you in another direction in life. Don't ignore the dissatisfaction you feel in life; it may just be a sign from God, the one you've been waiting for.

Another step in discovering your purpose is you must be open to listening to others. My husband Demetrius Scott absolutely lights up whenever he talks about music. Music and my husband are inseparable. He loves all types of music. Whenever I ride with him in the car, I look forward to all the variety of music he is going to play. That's his element. Don't let him play music from the 80's and 90's—we would have to ride all day because he will have that car jumping. He also has tremendous business sense and he has the potential to be very successful in business. I suggested to him once that God may perhaps be steering him in the direction of starting his own radio show. When I said that to him, he said, "You know, I've heard that from a lot of people." It's interesting that God not only shared the idea through me, but through several other people also. He does speak through other people.

Listening to what others say about your gifts can can be instrumental in steering you in the right direction in life: the direction of your divine purpose. For example, when someone notices or comments on one of your talents, take note of it because God might be trying to tell you something through that person. Remember that we are all God's workmanship and He speaks through each of us to reach His people. The Bible says this regarding listening to advice: "The way of fools seems right to them, but the wise listen to advice" (Proverbs 12:15).

Yes, there are plenty of times when we shouldn't listen to what others say; but when what some people say about us registers with our spirits and our passions, convictions, out gifting, and what God has already revealed to us, then their words may just a tool used by God to lead us into His purpose for our lives.

When God created you He also gifted you, so take notice of your gifts. Throughout my life, I never enjoyed playing basketball, and this is in light of the fact that I played basketball in school. It just wasn't a sport that I liked. But any opportunity that I had to speak to people or lead people or help people in any way, that always got my attention. Helping people and interacting with them made me excited. What are some of your gifts? What is it that you do that makes you glow? What is it that you would happily and gladly do all day long if you could or had to? I know what I can do all day long. I can stand in front of a classroom and teach from sun-up to sundown. Teaching is my passion. I can teach any age group and on any subject. I love to empower people. I'd do it all day, everyday if possible and would keep a smile on my face while doing it. Why? Because I love it! It's what I was created to do.

Have you ever considered your talents and gifts? Do you get a kick out of soccer? Are you a strategic thinker? A great listener? Can you motivate others to action with your words? Are you skilled at building things? I suggest making a list of the things and activities that interest you the most, things you excel in. Ask yourself, "What's the one thing that I do better than others?" This can clue you in on what is your God-given purpose; it's a good way to get clues as to what your divine gifting is.

The gifts God gives us are like little seeds planted inside of us; but in order for them to grow, we have to use them. This means if you can't identify the "seeds of gifting" God has planted inside of you then you should try doing new things to find out what your true interests are. Through this process, God will reveal more to you about who you are and how you can serve Him.

You must discover what your passions are. If I were to ask you what makes you angry, joyful, excited, and passionate, what would you say? Pay close attention to the things that move you emotionally; they may point you in the direction of your God-given passions. For me, just talking about Christ stirs me up. Talking about building the Kingdom of God stirs me up. Talking about empowering the weak and healing the sick stirs me up. When coupled with my talents, these passions point in the direction of my purpose, which is to communicate those things that deeply impact people on a spiritual and emotional level.

Pray and ask God to show you the things that move you and then make a list of these things. And keep in mind that God wants you to discover His purpose for your life more than you do.

Consider that your purpose is not just about you; it's about what God wants to do through you in the lives of others. If you ignore or neglect your sense of dissatisfaction and what others say about you, and you ignore your gifts and your passions, then you are not only betraying yourself but you're also betraying God since it is He who has called you to carry out a specific purpose in the earth, one that will impact not only you but the lives of others.

God is able to reveal your purpose to you, and He will…as you diligently seek after Him (Hebrew 11:6).

The Lord and his divine purposes for our lives are perfect although we are not. We are assailed by doubts and fears that many times keep us from living out the purpose of God in our lives, but we can overcome these assaults by consistently reading and studying God's Word so that our faith will be made stronger day by day. As we learn of God and pray to Him regularly, we'll become more embolden in our faith and confident in God to accomplish the great things He has called us to do through His power and in His name.

God desires to give you all the details about your purpose, your uniqueness, your gifts and passions, and reveal to you just how chosen you are!

BUT NONE OF THIS MAKES SENSE!

"You did not choose me, but I chose you and appointed you so that you might go and bear fruit--fruit that will last—and so that whatever you ask in my name the Father will give you."—John 15:16 (NIV)

CAN REMEMBER FEELING LIKE THE MAN THAT ONCE said, "I have a clock that tells me when to get up, but some days I need one to tell me why." I Love the book of Genesis because it explains to us why God created people. Part of God's reason for creating man has to do with His conflict with Satan and the fallen angels. Before Satan fell into sin, he wore God's seal of perfection. The Bible records,

"Look how you have fallen from the sky, O shining one, son of the dawn! You have been cut down to the ground, O conquer of the Nations! You said to yourself, 'I will climb up to the sky. Above the stars of El I will set up my throne. I will rule on the mountain on assembly on the remote slopes of Zaphon. I will climb up to the clouds: I will make myself like the most high!' But you were brought down to Sheol, to the remote slopes of the pit."—Isaiah 14:12-15 (NET)

When Satan rebelled and led a number of angelic forces in a war against God, God brought judgement on that creation resulting in chaos, emptiness, and darkness, which are spoken of in Genesis 1:2. In the recreated earth, God's purpose was to create a man on the earth that reflected His image. He would give this creation (mankind) dominion over the earth under His sovereign rule. It is clear that God put man on the earth to reflect His image and to rule over His creation on earth (Genesis 1:26, 28).

But let's go deeper! Who was God showing mankind off to? Who was around to behold the beauty of God's magnificent new creation? There was no one around before Adam and Eve. Only after other humans were born could they reflect God's image to one another, thus glorifying God. But this isn't the the full picture. The more complete answer would be that mankind was designed to be beheld and adored by the angelic host both good and evil. That was the only crowd around to marvel over the beauty of God's newest creation, the only creation created in God's very own image. I believe God placed mankind on the earth to have dominion in place of Satan.

The earth is the theater for God's ultimate victory over Satan and the fallen angels. Satan desires to defy God by attempting to run the earth; this is why he tried to get the first humans, Adam and Eve, to follow him in rebellion against God. When Adam and Eve fell into sin, God's purpose was temporarily thwarted and Adam and Eve came under the rule of Satan. Disobedience to the true and living God brings us into obedience with false gods.

Let's go a little deeper into this. God is doing a work on the inside of you, one that you cannot see with your natural eyes.

What's taking place at the present moment is Satan has managed to obtained the title and role as the ruler of this world as recorded in John 12:31, which says, "Now is the Judgement of this world: now the ruler of this world will be driven out." Also, Jesus mentioned in John 14:30, "I will not speak with you much longer, for the ruler of this world is coming. He has no power over me."

Although Satan has been recognized as the ruler of the world, God regained dominion over the earth through the death and resurrection of His Son, Jesus Christ, as explained in Ephesians 1:19-23, which reads:

"And what is the exceeding greatness of his power toward us who believe, according to the working of his mighty power, Which he wrought in Christ, when he raised him from the dead, and set him at his own right hand in heavenly places. Far above all principality, and power, and might,

> and dominion, and every name that is named, not only in this world, but also in that which is to come: And hath put all things under his feet, and gave him to be the head over all things to the church, which is his body, the fullness of him that filleth all in all."

Christ's resurrection was the driving force in the Apostle Paul's life. In raising Jesus from the dead, God did not merely reverse the natural process of decay, but He transcended it. He raised Jesus to be a completely new life-form, giving him a resurrection body. Not only was Jesus raised from the grave, but He was seated at the right hand of the Father in heaven, which is the place of authority from which He now reigns. Christ is above all creation, including men and angels; this indicates that He is infinitely superior to all but the Father and Holy Spirit in status. Jesus' ascension and exaltation after His crucifixion on the cross completed the resurrection event, providing hope for Believers being that Jesus Christ has now become the first-fruit for of God's new creation (those who are born again).

I love the fact that the Apostle Paul explains in Ephesians 1:22 that all things were put under the feet of Jesus after His ascension and exaltation. Yes! All things!! We don't have to be afraid of what Satan may try to do to us because all things are under Christ's feet. All we have to do is remain focused on Christ and follow through with all that God has called us to do because God has everything else under control.

You are probably asking, "How does Christ exercise His Dominion and authority in the earth since He is seated next to the Father in heaven?" In the book of Ephesians, Paul reveals to us that Christ's dominion is to be exercised through the people of God, the church (the body of Christ). The Believers are supposed to not only exercise God's dominion in the earth, but reflect God's image and likeness on the earth as well. I've found many parallels recorded in the book of Genesis and the book of Ephesians. For example, Adam is a type of Christ and Eve is a typology of the Church. Eve was taken from Adam in his sleep and given to him after he woke up—she was his bride, a part of his body. Likewise, the church was brought forth as a result of Christ's death and resurrection and was given to Him as His bride and is a part of His body, hence the body of Christ. Both Adam and Eve reflected God's Image. The church is the corporate "New man"—the head and body, bridegroom and bride—created in God's image to exercise dominion over Satan and his angels.

It is through the body of Christ that God is able to regain what He lost in the fall of Man in the Garden of Eden. Through each of us Believers, God is regaining what He lost piece by piece. This is why you are so important and valuable. But keep in mind that it is only through Christ Jesus that all is restored. It's only through Christ Jesus that we are able to exercise dominion over Satan and his forces.

God's plan for you and I is bigger than any of us could have previously suspected. His plan has been concealed for ages until now. Through the church God is revealing His multifaceted wisdom of God to the rulers and the authorities in the heavenly realms. This was according to the eternal purpose that He executed in the earth through Christ Jesus, our Lord, through whom we have boldness and access to the Father. We can execute God's plan in the earth because of Christ's faithfulness according to Ephesians 3:9-12.

The Apostle Paul is explaining his ministry in light of God's eternal purpose. In verse 9, he refers to God as "he who created all things." Why does Paul bring up God's creation at this point? It's because he is talking about God's purpose for His creation, which is to have a man on the earth who would reflect His image and exercise dominion over the earth. The church has been a central part of God's purpose in the earth historically as well as currently. So, if we are the church, then we play a crucial role in God's ultimate purpose. Through the church (which is on the inside of all of us as Believers), God's manifold wisdom will be made known ("manifold" means "multi-faceted or multicolored like a beautiful jewel"). The history of the Christian church and the unfolding drama of redemption is watched with avid interest by the principalities and powers, which is a reference to angels.

The Apostle Paul described the church (the body of Christ) as a divine agent and also a divine fellowship with a divine mandate. So, we, as Believers, have been given a divine mandate. "A mandate to do what?" you ask. We have a divine mandate to:

- live holy
- live out our God-given purposes
- exercise our authority and dominion in the earth
- and become all that God has purpose for us to become.

CHAPTER 6: BUT NONE OF THIS MAKES SENSE!

Let's talk. If you and I were created in God's image, what should we look like? Try to answer that question. Really, how should we look? The definition of "image" is "a representation of the external form of a person or thing in art." So, if I'm supposed to be a representation of God, then what should I look like? Let's look at some of God's attributes to find out the answer:

- God is strong
- God is powerful
- God is a creator
- God is a provider
- God cannot change

Think about some what God is like. Know that those are the things we should resemble. We should look like our God because He created us in His Image.

This is why God created you. You are chosen to reflect God in the earth realm. You are chosen by God to do great things in the earth. Through you, God has expose Satan and revealed that Satan's plan is inferior. God loves to show you off before Satan and his angels. This is why God has chosen you: He is demonstrating through your life how He rewards those who are obedient to Him. That's why God chose you to open that restaurant: He wants to reveal through you His love and power in that industry. Tat's why God Chose you to write that book: He wants to prove through you that Satan and his forces are losing and that God's people are the real winners because they succeed through the dominate power: God's power. You have been chosen to do the things that God placed in your heart to do. You have been chosen by God to represent Him in all things. You have been...

- Chosen to open the school
- Chosen to open the restaurant
- Chosen to be a doctor
- Chosen to be a teacher
- Chosen to build that empire
- Chosen to write that book
- Chosen to open that business
- Chosen to work with those who are less fortunate
- Chosen to be the go-to person in your family
- Chosen to own a bank
- Chosen to own that subdivision
- Chosen to own a credit business
- Chosen to own all of those different franchises
- Chosen to work in the White House
- Chosen to be in Corporate America
- Chosen to work for Congress
- Chosen to play football
- Chosen to play soccer
- Chosen to play basketball
- Chosen to sing
- Chosen to write music
- Chosen to build that bridge
- Chosen to develop that area/land
- Chosen to change the school board system
- Chosen to speak for minorities
- Chosen to work in law enforcement
- Chosen to work in the school system
- Chosen to work in a hospital

- Chosen to write grants
- Chosen to write up proposals
- Chosen to be a wedding planner
- Chosen to be a mentor

You have been chosen for that which God gifted you to do…and more.

In case you're wondering why didn't I include any of the five-fold ministries spoken of by the Apostle Paul (apostles, pastors, evangelists, teachers, and prophets), it's because God purposely stopped me from doing so because many within the body of Christ are stuck only on those gifts and callings. May within the body of Christ tend to believe God has only gifted His people to operate in those areas alone, which isn't the case. God wants to use us in other areas as well: in the marketplace, the corporate world, the entertainment industry, the arts, academia, etc. You have been chosen by God to showcase His power and reflect His image in many areas, not just in the church.

So go and get that job at the White House and allow God to move through you in order to execute His will in this country. God Chose you and He has placed within you greatness. Wherever God sends you, it's not you that's operating, it's the God in you that's operating.

God wants His creation to wake up and march forward throughout all the earth doing all that He created us to do for His Kingdom and glory! Wake-up! We are God's 21st century mouthpieces like Noah; we are His voices just as Moses was. God desires to use us today to accomplish His will in the earth. God is doing some phenomenal things in your life so that He can impact many others;

just be still and know that everything is working for your
good.

CHAPTER 7

NOW THAT YOU GOT MY ATTENTION

"From inside the fish Jonah prayed to the Lord his God. He said: 'In my distress I called to the Lord, and he answered me. From deep in the realm of the dead I called for help, and you listened to my cry. You hurled me into the depths, into the very heart of the seas, and the currents swirled about me; all your waves and breaker swept over me. I said, 'I have been banished from your sight; yet I will look again toward your holy temple.'"—Jonah 2:1-4

GOD GOT JONAH'S FULL UNDIVIDED ATTENTION WHILE he was in the belly of a whale. God is strategic when it comes to getting our attention. And like Jonah learned, it's important that we complete God's assignment for our lives even if we must do so out of fear or anger. Yes, I said it! Even if it's out of fear or anger!

God's assignment for your life may not be easy; Jonah's wasn't. God told him to go to a city named Nineveh and tell the people there to repent for their sinful and wicked deeds or else God was going to judge and destroy them all. Jonah didn't want to go and deliver this message to these people, so he decided instead to jump on a ship and go in the opposite direction of Nineveh to a city named Joppa.

Jonah didn't want to do what God instructed him to do. Jonah disobeyed God. While on the ship heading towards Joppa, a storm arose, one which endangered the lives of everyone onboard. The people on the ship began to inquire as to why the storm arose and speculate as to whether it was due to someone's actions. The question went from "Why is the storm here?" to "Who is God trying to punish with this storm?" At that point, Jonah stepped forward and told them that he was the cause of the storm—that God sent the storm as a punishment for his disobedience. The waters were growing more tumultuous by the minute; the waves beating even harder against the side of the ship. At that point, the men then asked Jonah, "What should we do with you to make the sea calm down for us?" Jonah suggested to them that they should just pick him up and throw him over the side of the ship and into the sea. At first, the men tried their best to get the ship back to land, but the force of the storm was too great; they then began to cry out to God, "Please do not let us die for taking this man's life!! Do not hold us accountable for killing this innocent man for you!! O Lord, we have done as you pleased!!" Then they took Jonah and threw him overboard into the sea, and immediately the raging sea became calm. Seeing this, the men greatly feared the Lord and offered a sacrifice to Him as well as made vows to Him. While Jonah was in the water, the Lord sent a big fish to swallow him alive. Jonah stayed in the fish's belly over the next three days and nights. While he was in the fish's belly, Jonah cried out to God and began confessing his sins and begging God for forgiveness. Jonah then promised to obey God from that point on. Listen to Jonah's prayer:

> "The engulfing waters threatened me, the deep surrounded me; seaweed was wrapped around my head. To the roots of the mountains I sank down the earth beneath barred me in forever. But you, Lord my God brought my life up from the pit."—Jonah 2:5-6

God will get your attention just like he got Jonah's. Whatever He has to do, He will do it; and in the end, you'll end-up in the same position as Jonah, crying and repenting to God while begging Him to rescue you so that you can go and obey His will. You'll be praying prayers just like this one, which Jonah offered up to God:

> When my life was ebbing away I remembered you, Lord, and my prayer rose to you, to your holy temple. Those who cling to worthless idols turn away from God's love for them. But I, with shouts of grateful praise, will sacrifice to

you. What I have vowed I will make good. I will say, "Salvation comes from the Lord." And the Lord commanded the fish, and it vomited Jonah onto dry land. (Jonah 2:7-10)

God heard Jonah's prayers and commanded the fish to swim to shore and vomit Jonah out onto the land. Then the Lord spoke to Jonah again and told him to go to Nineveh to deliver His message to the people there. This time, Jonah obeyed the word of the Lord and went to Nineveh. When Jonah arrived in Nineveh, he delivered this message to the people, which God gave him to deliver: "Forty days from now Nineveh will be destroyed!!!" Jonah finally obeyed God and did what he was instructed to do.

Again, God will do whatever He feels is necessary in order to gain your full undivided attention. God got my attention the hard way. Looking back at your life, it may amaze you when noticing all of the things God had to do just to get your attention, when looking at all of the experiences He had to take you through just to get you to look up and finally surrender to His will.

After my first divorce, I quickly remarried. Remember when I explained in chapter two that I was angry with God because He didn't restore my first marriage? Well, out of anger I made a few reckless decisions. It hadn't even been a year after my divorce that I remarried. I didn't marry this time for love, for security, for protection, or for God's sake; I remarried only for the sake of…sex. Yep, I said it! Sex!!! There are many people today who marry for all of the wrong reasons; sex is certainly one of them. When I remarried, I was an ordained evangelist; therefore, I was concerned about what people might say about me—I didn't want them saying that I was a hypocrite; so I married quickly to not make my union look like sin in the people's eyes. Also, I remarried quickly because I didn't want to complete the assignment, the vision that God gave me, all alone. I wanted a partner to share in the heavy load with me.

God got my attention before I remarried, but He really got my attention after I remarried. After remarrying, I enjoyed traveling around the country, especially since I had never been anywhere outside of Florida. During this time, God was downloading all of this information into my spirit concerning His vision and assignment for me, which consisted of His divine purpose for my life—His reason for creating me. And as much as I wanted God to take back His assignment and just let me be, just let me do my own thing, He wouldn't.

I impulsively remarried out of disobedience. I was ready to do God's will, but I didn't want to do it His way: all alone. God may be sending you to where He wants you to be all alone. Truthfully, some of the people you think you need in order to accomplish what God wants you to do, you really don't need them. I grew into a needy individual, thinking I always had to have someone in order to accomplish my purpose in life. But thanks be to God that He delivered me from that mentality! Whenever God gives you an assignment, all you need in order to successfully accomplish that task is God's guidance—He will connect you to those He has set aside to help you carry out His will for your life.

My future was altered and the plans of God for

my life were slowed down due to me listening to my flesh rather than listening to the Holy Spirit. Rather than seeking God, I decided to enter into a second marriage. Disobedience will destroy you if you don't repent. My disobedience towards God almost destroyed my life. My actions led me to a place where I began to experience the same exact feelings that I experienced after my mother died: suicide, depression, low self-esteem, abandonment, etc.

When you disobey God, you open yourself up to things that are not from God. My act of disobedience caused me seven years of pain and suffering. I almost lost my identity within those seven years. I almost lost my children within those seven years. Now, don't misinterpret what I'm saying. My disobedience was mine alone. I couldn't blame anyone else for my actions.

Whenever we disobey God, it's important that we take full responsibility for the things that we do and not blame others. No, it wasn't my second husband's fault; it was my fault. Let me say that again: It wasn't my second husband's fault; it was my fault. Why? Because God told me not to remarry at the time, I chose chose to do what I wanted to do anyway. I wanted what I wanted and I got it! But not only did I get what I wanted, which was that man, but I also got what came with him. I do believe that the whole time I was in that marriage, God was working behind the scenes to get me back on the right track. I believe God allowed this marriage to fail deliberately because it was a union that wasn't ordained and approved by Him. He was working to get my attention again.

Seven years of pain and suffering certainly made me turn back to God. When I tell you I began to pull on God in a major way during those seven years, I'm not kidding. The pain from that second marriage to my prayer life to another level. I found myself buried so deep in the Word of God and in prayer that I was no earthly good to anyone.

Those seven years birthed a new level of intercession in me. Those seven years caused me to love God in a way that words could never explain. For years, I would put my children to sleep at night, and then sleep in my prayer closet just to feel God's presence. Seventy-five percent of the time my second husband and I were married, he didn't live in the home with me. God certainly used this as an opportunity to get my attention.

Within those seven years, God not only took my intercession to another level, but He took me to a new level of intimacy with Him. I was more like I acquired a direct one-on-one with Him. It seemed as if during my hardest times, that's when God began to speak the loudest in my life. These were painful moments; shameful moments. It was a horrible marriage. I was 28yrs old, in my second marriage, but was still practically a single parent and feeling as if I really didn't have a family. No one was there for me. Holidays were a blur for me. I desperately missed my mother during this season. My father was living, but I never had a close relationship with hm, so I couldn't turn to him. Don't get me wrong! I loved my father with everything within me and I believed he loved me, too, even though I never heard him say it or saw him demonstrate it. When I did visit my father, his smile would express everything to me that his mouth would not say. Although he's dead now, I still miss his smile. It would take me another book just to explain everything that I felt about my father and all that I desired from him—that book is coming soon. God did bless me with the opportunity to lead my father to Christ. The bastard child, the outside child that my father had, happened to be the one God used to lead him to Christ.

Back to my earlier point of feeling alone: I wanted someone to hold me and tell me that everything was going to be okay. I needed someone to tell me that I wasn't losing my mind. But no one came. So my prayer closet was all I had. There, God wrapped His loving arms around me and said to me, "If you would just trust me, I'm going to give you your greatest heart's desires." I said,

"Lord, do you promise?"

"I promise," He replied. "I'm going to do amazing thing through you. A nation will know you were in contact with me. You won't be able to explain all that I'm going to do for you and for your children and for their their children and so on." God even revealed to me that I was going to go through another divorce, and that if I obeyed Him and didn't allow my flesh to get in the way, He would send the right man into my life.

I trusted God; and as time went by, everything He promised me began to unfold. Although still married, I was basically again, just me and my babies. My babies became my reason for pushing forward and not giving up in life. I asked God to have His way in our lives, and He did. I remember saying to God one day, "Okay, you have my attention! Now what?"

I will never forget what happened next! One Saturday morning, God woke me up and told me pack light, to get in my van, buckle my four kids up, and drive north until He said stop. I drove and drove until I ended up in Georgia. He then told me to take the kids out of the van, make them take off their shoes, and all of us together give Him praise. We held hand and began to praise God right there at that rest stop. My kids were young at the time: Tremonte was 10yrs old, Vernisha was 8yrs old, Robert was 6yrs old, and Isaiah was 5yrs old. They had no clue what God was doing, but they where smiling and excited because they saw the excitement in my eyes—I knew God was about to do something incredible in our lives.

We were in College Park, Georgia, and God told me to just ride around and get use to the scenery. I was so afraid because I didn't know anyone there. I had no family or friends there; absolutely no one. God then told me to check into a hotel, which I did. After I fed the kids and put them to sleep that night, God sent me to a passage of Scripture in His Word, which He told me to read immediately. It was a passage about Abraham. It read:

"The Lord had said to Abram, 'Go from your country, you people and your fathers household to the land I will show you. I will make you into a great nation, and I will bless you: I will make your name great, and you will be a blessing. I will bless those that bless you and whoever curses you I will curse: and all peoples on the earth will be blessed through you.' So Abram went, as the Lord had told him: and Lot went with him. Abram was seventy five years old when he sent him out of Haran."—Genesis 12:1-4

After reading this passage of Scripture, I began to cry and praise God, thanking Him for what He was about to do in my life. God immediately said to me, "Daughter, only have faith and trust that I am going to do a mighty work through you." I then gave God another yes from the depths of my soul. After that, I began to witness God's great plan begin to unfold right before my very eyes.

I know that God is speaking to you today. Although it may look like everything around you is falling apart, I want you to stand still and listen to what God is saying about your situation:

> "And we know that all things work together for the good of them that love the lord god, to them who are the called according to his purpose."—Romans 8:28

To you, it may seem as if everything is falling apart when in reality God is simply rearranging some things so that everything will be together in your life the way it supposed to be. Look up and trust God because He's still in control! God is trying to get your attention; and once He has it, He will give you all that you need to move to the next level in your life. Remember what He said in His Word:

> "The lions may grow weak and hungry, but those that seek the Lord lack no good thing."—Psalms 34:10

> "And my God will fully supply your every need

according to his glorious riches in Messiah Jesus."—Philippians 4:10

It's about to open up for you! Activate your faith now! No more wavering! No more being afraid! Open up your mouth and tell God, "God, I'm ready and you have my attention!! Now what?!!" Know that God is faithful and just and He will tell you what He wants you to do next. He did it for me just as He has for so many others. As His Word declares:

> "Now faith is confidence in what we hope for and assurance about what we do not see."—Hebrew 11:1

> "And without faith it is impossible to please God, because anyone who comes to him must first believe that he exists and that he rewards those who earnestly seek him."—Hebrews 11:6

You were chosen for this! Now is the time for you to rise up and allow God to birth out of you everything that He impregnated you with!

CHOSEN

CHAPTER 8

LET'S GO! A NATION IS WAITING ON YOU

"But when he, the Spirit of truth, comes, he will guide you into all the truth. He will not speak on his own: he will speak only what he hears, and he will tell you what is yet to come."—John 16:13

"But you will receive power when the Holy Spirit comes on you: and you will be my witness in Jerusalem and in Judea, and in Samaria and to the ends of the earth."—Acts 1:8

It's that time! "Time for what?" you ask. It's time for you to get up and go forward into what God called you to do! Now that you know why it's important that you obey God and get out of that cave of fear, realizing that God has chosen you for an awesome purpose in this earth, it's time for you to move! Don't delay! You were chosen for this and that settles it! God has gifted and anointed you for such a time as this. You don't have to be afraid of starting on the path, the journey that your feet were predestined by God to walk. Everyone had to start somewhere. Your starting point is right here, right now!

Today, you have a choice: You can choose to be like one of the individuals we discussed in the first chapter. Remember in Matthew chapter twenty-two where Jesus talked about the two groups of invitees: the first group being the notable guests who didn't heed the master of the house's the invitation, but instead, disregarded it and continued on with their busy schedules and their own agenda's and ended up missing out on the banquet; and the other group being the group that heeded the call and accepted the invitation and became partakers in the wedding feast. Don't be like that first group and miss out on what God has for you. Don't be too busy to hear God's voice and surrender to His purpose and plan for your life. Wake up and listen to what He is trying to tell you. You may not have a clue of just how important it is for you to grab ahold of what God is saying and what He is doing on the inside of you. He is pulling on you because He is trying to bring His purpose and plan into fruition in your life, and His plan is MAGNIFICENT!!!

In the previous chapter, I explained to you how God got my attention; but now, I need to explain to you what He did after He finally got my attention. God began to speak to me over the next few days, "Daughter, go back to Florida and put your house up for sale and pack because I'm relocating you within 90 days." I obeyed God and I went back to Florida and told my job, which I had faithfully been on for eight years, that I wouldn't be returning after the summer—I was a paraprofessional for the Broward County School System. I then put my house on the market as God commanded and I began packing up everything in my home. What's amazing is I found a house in Georgia online. Never had I seen the house before. I didn't know anything about the area. I was simply following the Holy Spirit's guidance. The Holy Spirit instructed me to get that house, which I did. I was leaving a job where I had full benefits and security to go where I had never gone before. But God said go!

My departure date to leave Florida was fast approaching. About two weeks before my scheduled departure, everything that could go wrong did. It was a disaster. I couldn't close the deal on my house in Florida. Although broken, the marriage to my second husband was still intact and I was unsure as to what I needed to do moving forward regarding it. Do I remain in it? Do I approach him about a divorce? What? My head was spinning. And yet, in the midst of all of the confusion and chaos, I heard the Holy Spirit's voice telling me, "It's time to go! No delays! No distractions! No stopping!" When I heard the Holy Spirit's voice, I immediately I got myself together and continued to pack my stuff while preparing to leave. I didn't want to disobey God because of fear.

Dearly beloved, it seemed as if God was pulling me into my destiny even without my permission. It was as if God was dragging me by my legs out of the past and into my future. And yes, this process was difficult and stressful, but it was all worth it in the end. Everything worked out in the end.

That departure date had finally arrived. It was time to leave Florida and relocate permanently to Georgia. There I was that morning, looking like a deer caught in the headlights. I was so afraid. My kids and I all got into the van and drove off without any real understanding of what God was doing. Still, I kept hearing the whisper into my spirit, "Go."

Now watch how God works: We finally arrived at the house in Georgia. Once we got there and saw the house, we were all crying with joy and excited because the pictures on the web didn't do the house justice. My children thought they were in heaven! The house was huge! The landlord was so excited to meet me; and little did I know God had already prepared her for my arrival. Out of her own mouth she said this was a divine hook up… and it really was. Originally, the house was for rent, but once I expressed to her that I was interested in buying a home, she said to me, "I already know and I already have your home you will purchase." No one can't tell me that this couple weren't angels. Everything I needed, God provided through them. It was simply amazing! In less than 90 days, my house in Florida was sold and we purchased our new home in Hiram, Georgia. I was able to raise my children in an awesome community.

I'm trying to show you that once you obey God, God will take care of the rest. He'll see to it that everything you need is taken care of and you're provided for. God did it for me and my kids in a major way. He also kept reminding me that Georgia was just one of my assignments; therefore, He didn't want me to get too comfortable. I began to develop an even greater confidence when it came to following God, knowing that He has my back and that He won't let me down. And as I continued to walk in obedience to His voice, I began to grow stronger and wiser with each passing moment.

I can truly say to you today that I am about my Father's business, and I want you to join me. The Father is calling you higher. Come and experience all that He has for you. Don't die without completing your purpose in the earth! You have too much to do! Let's go!! You are ready now!!

REMEMBER: YOU WERE CHOSEN FOR THIS!!!